Here are ten questions to think about during Hanukkah.

1 What's the difference between the dreidle that kids play with in the United States and the dreidle that kids play with in Israel?

5 Why was Yehudah (Judah) given the nickname "hammer"?

8 What are the names of the five sons of Mattityahu ben Yohanan?

2 What are two meanings for the word Hanukkah?

9 How did Yehudah the Maccabee destroy the greatest generals that Antiochus sent against him?

3 What is the story of Hannah and her seven sons?

6 What sweet food do the Jews in Israel eat instead of latkas?

4 What two things – exactly three years apart– happened on the 25th of the Hebrew month of Kislev?

7 What evil decrees did King Antiochus Epiphanes try to force the Jews to accept?

10 Why is it important to light the menorah so that people in the street can see the lights?

Text Copyright © 1998 PITSPOPANY PRESS INC.
Cover Illustration © 1998 Ron Barrett
Inside Illustrations © 1998 Don Channen
Design: Benjie Herskowitz

REVISED AND EXPANDED SECOND EDITION
Original title: Uh! Oh! Hanukkah

ISBN: 0-943706-27-0

PITSPOPANY PRESS titles may be purchased for educational or special sales by contacting:
Marketing Director, Pitspopany Press, 40 East 78th Street, Suite 16D, New York, N.Y. 10021.
Fax: (212) 472-6253

Printed in Hong Kong

The ENERGIZING

Hanukkah
Story For Children

BY CHAIM MAZO
COVER ILLUSTRATION BY RON BARRETT
ILLUSTRATED BY DON CHANNEN

PITSPOPANY
NEW YORK ◆JERUSALEM

Table of Contents

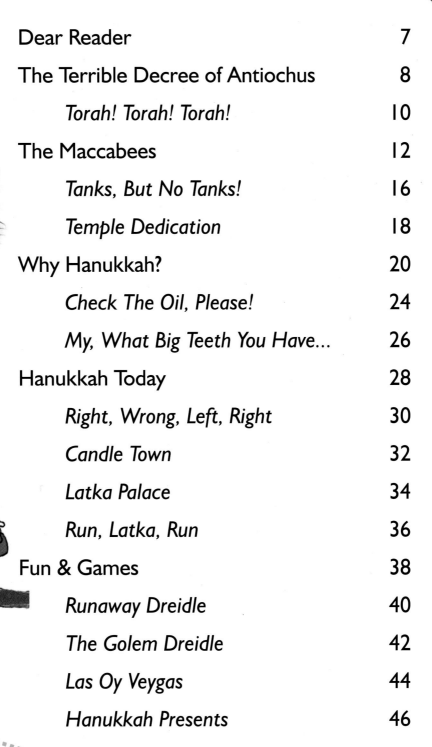

Dear Reader:

This book flits freely from fun to fact.

The *Can you find?* illustrations are filled with comic characters rushing around madly, trying to get somewhere or do something that, we are sure, will leave you laughing. The hidden objects are sometimes quite hard to find. At the Pitspopany Press testing center, we found that the younger readers (eight and nine year olds) often found the hidden objects in the illustrations quicker than the older readers. The average time for all age groups to find all the hidden objects was 27 minutes. See how well you can do.

While all the illustrations tell parts of the Hanukkah story, we wanted to give you a fuller appreciation of this miraculous holiday. So, there are sections that deal with the history of the Jews in Israel at that time, what happened during the wars between the Maccabees and the Greeks, how the miracle of Hanukkah occurred, how to light Hanukkah candles, and even how to play the game of dreidle.

For those of you who have not read some of our other titles, such as JERUSALEM 3000: Kids Discover the City of Gold! (a wonderfully illustrated book about Jerusalem), TELL IT FROM THE TORAH (Torah facts and fun), and THE JEWISH CHILDREN'S BIBLE (all the stories in the Bible vividly illustrated), we should mention that we refer to dates before the calendar year one, with the letters B.C.E. – Before the Common Era. We also use the original Hebrew names of the people in the Bible and in the Hanukkah story. So, Judah the Maccabee is called Yehudah the Maccabee in our book.

Now, take out your dreidles and get ready to spin through these pages of facts and fun.

On your mark! Get set! Spinnnnnnnnnnnnnnnnnnnn!

The Terrible Decree of Antiochus

In the year 168 B.C.E., over 2,100 years ago, Antiochus Epiphanes, the king of the Greek Empire (also known as the Seleucid Empire), decided to wipe out the Jewish religion.

The first thing the king did was to have his general, Apollonius, attack the Jews of Jerusalem on Shabbat, when they were peacefully resting and enjoying themselves. Many Jews were killed. Others ran away and their houses were given to the Greeks and Syrians living in Israel.

But that was not enough for the cruel King Antiochus. He then passed terrible decrees, saying:

1) Jews are forbidden to learn Torah.

2) Jews are forbidden to worship God in the Temple in Jerusalem.

3) Jews are forbidden to keep the Shabbat.

4) Jews are forbidden to circumcise their sons.

5) Jews are forbidden to eat kosher food.

Special guards were sent to make sure the Jews carried out the decrees. If they worshipped God, they were killed.

Everyone had to worship the Greek god Zeus and other idols.

It's hard to believe that things could get worse, but they did. On the 25th of the Hebrew month of Kislev, exactly three years before the Maccabees would actually defeat the Greek armies [more about this later], Antiochus had the Syrians and Greeks go into the Temple in Jerusalem and bring sacrifices to Zeus. Many Jews were forced to join and sacrifice to this idol – some were also forced to eat pork.

But there were those who decided they would rather die than worship an idol. A Jewish woman named Hannah, and her seven sons, were told to bow down to Zeus. But none of Hannah's children would agree to bow down. The cruel Greek officer had each child killed. Finally, the youngest child was told to pick up a beautiful ring that the officer dropped in front of the idol. But the child refused to pick up the ring. He knew it would look like he was bowing down to Zeus. So he was killed too. Hannah then went up to the top of the Temple wall and threw herself to the ground. She wanted to show everyone that it was better to die than to bow down to idols.

After that, the Syrians and Greeks began to kill the Jews and destroy their houses everywhere in Israel. It was one of the worst times in Jewish history.

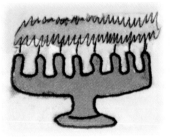

Then, in the small town of Modiin....

TORAH! TORAH! TORAH!

The Greeks wore fancy armor and conquered many lands. They outnumbered the Maccabees ten-to-one. Yet, the Maccabees won battle after battle. How did they do it? Was it their fancy footwork? Sharp spearing? Jewjitsu? What do you think? (See title for hint.)

Can You Find?

Cup

Bones

False Teeth

Meatball on Fork

The Maccabees

In the year 167 B.C.E. there lived in the city of Modiin an elderly Kohen (priest) called Mattityahu ben Yohanan. He was a member of the Hashmonayim family. Mattityahu had five sons: Yohanan, Shimon, Yehudah, Yonatan, and Eliezer.

One day soldiers of the wicked King Antiochus came into the city of Modiin. They put an idol in the center of the city and commanded everyone to sacrifice to the idol. Since Mattityahu was the most famous person in the town, the soldiers told him to show everyone how important it was to listen to the king and bring a sacrifice. Of course, Mattityahu refused, saying, "We shall not follow the laws of the king. We shall remain true to our fathers and our faith."

But another Jew stepped forward with a sacrifice to the idol. When Mattityahu saw this, he ran over and killed the man. Then, together with his sons, he attacked and killed the Greek soldiers, and broke the idol.

The revolt against King Antiochus had begun. Soon,

thousands of Jews joined Mattityahu and his sons. They began to attack the Greeks and Syrians throughout the Land of Israel. Unfortunately, the elderly Mattityahu died soon after the revolt began. But he commanded his children to continue the fight against Antiochus and his soldiers.

Yehudah, whose English name is Judah, became the leader of the Jewish army. He was given the Hebrew nickname, "Maccabee," which means hammer. Like a hammer, he pounded his enemies and drove them out of the country. For a short time it looked like Yehudah would easily win the war and free the Land of Israel and the Temple from Greek rule. But Antiochus had large armies. He sent an army of many thousands to destroy Yehudah and his fighters. The Greek army was led by Antiochus' most famous generals, Nicanor and Gorgias.

The people of Israel were afraid. The Greek army was much, much greater in number than the Jewish army. But Yehudah the Maccabee knew that God was on the side of the Jews. He gathered all his troops at Mitzpah and told them to fast and pray to God. He reminded them of what the Syrians had done to Jerusalem and the holy Temple. He also told them what the Greeks and Syrians would do to their families if the Jewish army lost. Then Yehudah said that all those who were afraid of the Greeks should leave the army. He did not want the soldiers who were too afraid to fight, to make the other soldiers afraid as well.

One night, the Greek army decided to attack. They knew where the Jews were camped and thought that if they launched a sneak attack against Yehudah and his men, they would be able to destroy them. But the Greek generals made a big mistake. They left half their army at their base. They were certain that they would not need so many soldiers to defeat the Jews.

The Greeks raced to Mitzpah. But Yehudah saw what they were doing and quietly took his soldiers and circled around the Greeks, attacking their base and killing many enemy soldiers. When the Greek generals could not find the Jewish army, they went back to their camp. To their surprise, they found Yehudah and his army waiting for them. The Greeks were so surprised that they left all their valuables and animals, and ran away. Yehudah had won one of the biggest battles ever against the Greeks.

By the year 165 B.C.E., Yehudah and his men had destroyed all the armies that Antiochus had sent to destroy the people of Israel. On the 25th day of Kislev, the same day that

three years earlier the worship of Zeus had taken place, the Temple was recaptured by the Maccabees and the sacrifices to God were renewed.

But the war against the Greeks was not over. For the next two years, the Maccabees, as the Jewish army was called, fought many battles against the Greeks. And they did not always win. In a battle near Jerusalem, the Greeks attacked using elephants as tanks to trample the Jewish soldiers. Eliezer, one of Yehudah's brothers, fought his way through the Greeks until he crawled underneath one of the elephants. With a mighty heave, he drove his sword into the elephant. The elephant went wild. Eliezer could not run away fast enough to avoid being crushed by the elephant as it fell to the ground. Despite this act of bravery, the Syrians won the battle.

Nevertheless, in 163 B.C.E., the Syrians offered the Jews a peace treaty which the Jews accepted. All the evil decrees of Antiochus Epiphanes were dissolved and the Jewish people were once again able to worship God as they pleased.

TANKS, BUT NO TANKS!

Before tanks there were elephants. The Maccabees had to use special tactics to conquer these giant gray Greek gargantuans. Getting some squeaky mice to scare the elephants helped, but Yehudah and his men had some other secret weapons too. How many can you spot?

Can You Find?

Bucket

UH! OH!

Peanut

Axe

Flower Pot

TEMPLE DEDICATION

After many battles, the Maccabees recaptured their Temple. The Levites once again struck-up the band, and sang the Psalms. Thousands came to celebrate, and they all found room...even without reserved seating.

Can You Find?

Upside Down Meatball

Table Sign

Musical Note

Elephant

Why Hanukkah?

The Talmud asks the question, "Why is this holiday called Hanukkah?" The answer lies in the word Hanukkah, which means *They rested on the 25th* of the Hebrew month of Kislev. That is when the Jews were able to rest from fighting the Greeks. Hanukkah also means to rededicate or renew.

On the 25th of Kislev, in the year 165 B.C.E., the Maccabees entered the Temple in Jerusalem. They found signs of idol worship everywhere. The Greeks had even erected idols and altars in the very heart of the Temple, where only the Kohen Gadol (the High Priest) was permitted to enter on Yom Kippur.

As they looked around, the Maccabees realized that the Greeks had either stolen or used the beautiful gold, silver, and copper utensils of the Temple for their idol worship. People cried as they remembered how beautiful the Temple once looked, and how splendid the daily service in the Temple had been.

Now began the process of cleaning up and rededicating the Temple.

The first thing Yehudah the Maccabee wanted to do was to light the Menorah in the Temple. Lighting the Menorah was the duty of the Kohen Gadol. Until the Greeks set up idols in the Temple, the Kohen Gadol had always performed the daily Menorah lighting. By lighting the Menorah again, the Kohen Gadol would be announcing to everyone that the Temple service was being renewed.

The Menorah was also the only major object in the Temple made from a single piece of pure gold. Just as the Menorah was made of pure gold, so too the oil that was poured into the Menorah had to be pure olive oil. Unfortunately, the Greeks had used the pure oil for their idol worship. Now, according to Jewish law, the oil was considered tainted, impure.

So, the search was on to find pure oil.

The Maccabees searched high and low, but in the end, all they could find was one small sealed jar of pure oil. While they were happy to find the oil, the Maccabees were also a bit worried because it would take eight days to make new oil from olives, and the jar looked as though it held barely enough oil for one day.

But Yehudah was sure that just as God had shown them this jar of oil, God would also provide more oil when they needed it.

And that's exactly what happened.

The little jar of oil lasted for eight days. Miraculously, no matter how much oil they poured into the Menorah, the jar of oil remained full.

Think About This!

The Rabbis debated how the miracle of the oil occurred.

One group of Rabbis believed that what the Maccabees did was divide the oil that was in the jar into eight parts. Every day the Kohen Gadol poured oil into only one branch of the Menorah. That way at least part of the Menorah was lit until more oil could be made.

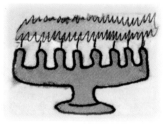

But then, you might ask, what was the miracle? If they divided the oil into eight parts – one for each day – then of course they had enough for one branch of the Menorah to be lit each day! The answer, according to the Rabbis, is that although they divided the oil into eight parts, when they poured the oil, they found that each part held enough oil to fill all eight branches of the Menorah. So, the Menorah was completely lit the entire eight days!

Other Rabbis felt that the Maccabees poured all the oil into the Menorah the very first day. The miracle was that the oil continued to burn for all eight days.

But if there was enough oil for one day, then the miracle was that the oil lasted an extra seven days, not eight days!

The answer to this may be that actually finding the little jar of oil was the miracle of the first day. Or, maybe there was only enough oil to light one branch of the Menorah on the first day, but certainly not all eight branches on the first day.

CHECK THE OIL, PLEASE!

The Greeks used all the Temple oil for idol worship. There was no pure oil left. The Maccabees were very depressed. But then the oil checkers found a small jar of oil. Miraculously, the oil lit the Menorah for eight days. Question: Who put all those olives in that little bitty jar?

Can You Find?

Lunch box

Chess Rook

Bowling Ball

Section of Pipe

MY, WHAT BIG TEETH YOU HAVE...

Izzy is off to grandmother's house. She's anxiously waiting for him to bring the jar of olive oil so she can light her Hanukkah menorah. But Izzy has to be careful to follow the dreidle signs to grandmother's house. UH! OH! Can you help Izzy avoid the obstacles in his path?

Can You Find?

Match stick

Periscope

Green Menorah

Sea Monster Tail

UH! OH!

Hanukkah Today

 The miracle of Hanukkah was a miracle of light and oil, so many of the laws and customs have to do with light and oil. Of course there are other laws and customs that are based on the fact that the Greeks tried to destroy Judaism. And then there are a few customs which are found in one country and not another.

But one thing is for sure. Today, Jews throughout the world celebrate Hanukkah by lighting the menorah at home. It is a symbol of the light of Judaism that every Jew carries within him.

Candle Lighting

1) Since the Maccabees used oil to light the Menorah in the Temple, oil is the preferred method for candle lighting, but wax candles are fine too.

2) The menorah is always lit at night.

3) Starting with one candle on the first night of Hanukkah, every night an additional candle is lit until there are eight candles burning on the last night of Hanukkah.

4) Every night, the candles are placed into the menorah starting from the right side and moving toward the left side of the menorah. The candles are lit, however, starting from the left

side and moving toward the right side of the menorah.

5) On the first night of Hanukkah, three blessings are recited. On all other nights only two blessings are recited.

6) The extra candle usually placed on the side of the menorah is the *Shames,* the servant candle. It is used to light the other candles.

7) After the candle is lit, the flame should burn for at least 30 minutes into the night.

8) In some homes it is customary to light one menorah for the whole family. In other homes each person, even the little children, has his own menorah.

9) The menorah should be seen by those walking in the street. In this way, when you light the menorah, you proudly display your belief in the miracle of Hanukkah.

Latkas and Soofganiyot

Fried potato pancakes, called by their Yiddish name *latkas,* are the holiday food of Hanukkah. Traditionally, they are served with sour cream or applesauce, and eagerly devoured by young and old alike.

In Israel, the holiday food of choice is jelly donuts, called in Hebrew *soofganiyot.* Fried in oil, these sugar-covered delights are filled with either jam or butterscotch. Soofganiyot are available everywhere in Israel from about one month before Hanukkah until well after Hanukkah.

RIGHT, WRONG, LEFT, RIGHT

On Hanukkah it pays to know your right from your left. Remember, you put the candles into the menorah from right to left, but you light them from left to right. If you are standing opposite someone lighting candles, his left is your right, and your right is his left, although your left is always your left...right?

Can You Find?

Cap

Bow Tie

Net

Coffee Pot

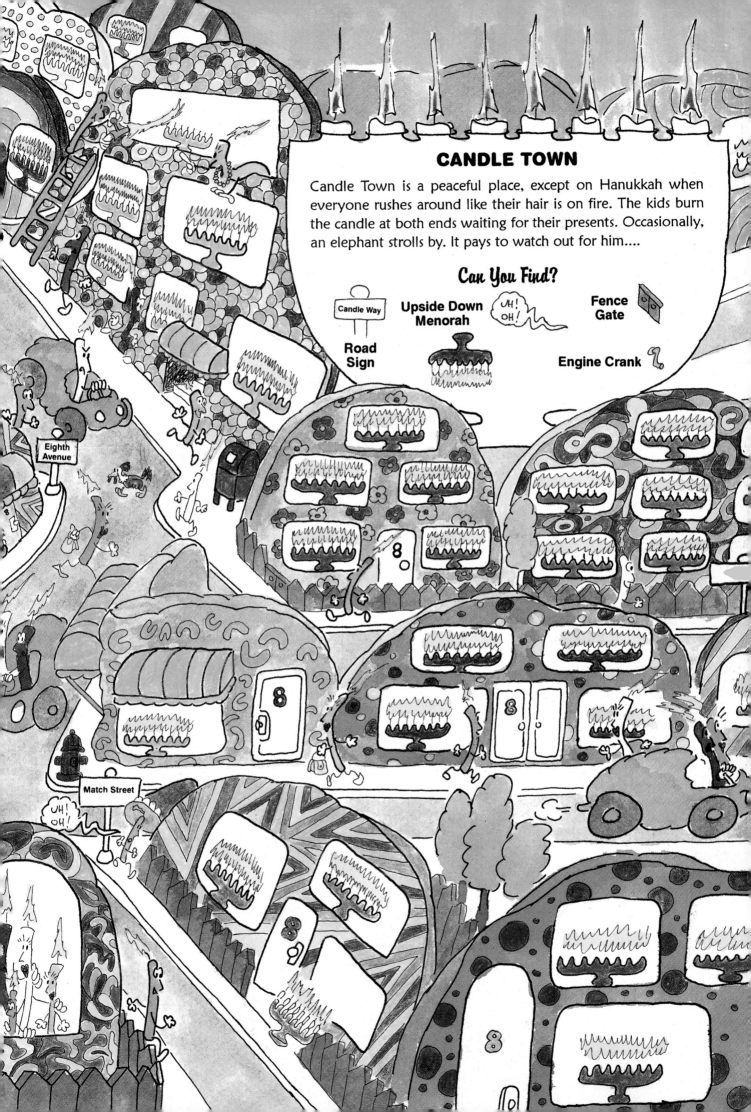

CANDLE TOWN

Candle Town is a peaceful place, except on Hanukkah when everyone rushes around like their hair is on fire. The kids burn the candle at both ends waiting for their presents. Occasionally, an elephant strolls by. It pays to watch out for him....

Can You Find?

Road Sign

Upside Down Menorah

Fence Gate

Engine Crank

LATKA PALACE

You need lots of oil to make a really good latka. Applesauce and sour cream are great side dishes for dipping latkas. But the latka connoisseur always eats her latka straight, using only the finest napkins to catch the oil oozing down her chin. The customers at Latka Palace come from places "no man has gone before," to savor these edible frisbees.

Can You Find?

Ant

UH! OH!

Potato Head with 2 ears on one side

Hat

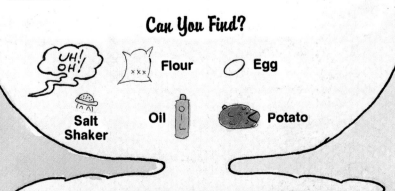

RUN, LATKA, RUN!

Do too many chefs scare the food? Some of these dishes just don't want to be served. See those latkas trying to escape? But don't worry, the ingredients for more latkas are around somewhere.

Can You Find?

UH!
OH!

Flour

Egg

Salt
Shaker

Oil

Potato

Fun & Games

Kids love Hanukkah for many reasons, but one of the best reasons is that they get to play dreidle. A dreidle is a spinning top with personality. Every dreidle has four Hebrew letters on it:

Nun, Gimel, Hay, Shin.

Each letter stands for a word. Together, the words mean:

A great miracle happened there (in Israel)!

In Israel, where the miracle of Hanukkah actually took place, the dreidles have these four letters on them

Nun, Gimel, Hay, Pey

Each letter stands for a word too. Together, the words mean:

A great miracle happened here!

There are many ways to play dreidle. One of the most common is for everyone to sit in a circle. Each person puts a coin (some kids use candy, or even basketball cards) into the middle of the circle. If someone wins all the coins in the circle, each player has to put another coin into the circle.

The first player spins the dreidle. If it lands on the letter

Gimel, the player takes everything in the middle of the circle. If the dreidle lands on the letter Hay, the player takes half of everything in the middle of the circle. If the dreidle lands on the letter Shin (or Pey), the player loses a turn. If the dreidle lands on the letter Nun, the player has to put another coin into the circle.

Each person gets to spin the dreidle. When one person has won all the coins, he or she is the winner.

Hanukkah Gelt

The Yiddish word, *gelt*, which means money, can be found in almost any American dictionary today. Since Hanukkah is a family holiday, many parents, grandparents, aunts, and uncles make it a practice to give presents to the kids in their family. These presents can take the form of toys and books or Hanukkah gelt – coins which the children will use to buy candies or sometimes to play dreidle. Hanukkah gelt also comes as gold and silver covered chocolate coins which melt in your mouth – and in your hands.

Some families give presents to the children every night of Hanukkah. Others give presents only on the first night of Hanukkah. But the custom of playing dreidle and eating latkas goes on for all eight days.

RUNAWAY DREIDLE!

Hanukkah dreidles love to spin their tops. But after a long, hard day of twirling and whirling, it's comforting to know that there's a dreidle doctor on call. The dreidles just zig-zag on in, get fixed up, and zoom out again to spin, spin, spin!

Can You Find?

Hammer

Dreidle with Glasses

Stopwatch

Four Leaf Clover

THE GOLEM DREIDLE

Before Superman, there was – and still is – the Golem; a mud-made super hero ready to help the Jewish people whenever they are in trouble. But don't try to make one yourself. You have to know just the right words to create him, wake him...and control him.

Can You Find?

Hamburger Hat

Two-headed Spear

Roller Skates

Mud pie

HANUKKAH PRESENTS

Everyone loves getting gifts, especially on Hanukkah. It's exciting to open a brightly wrapped gift, pull away the ribbons, and grab what's inside...unless, of course, it grabs you first!

Can You Find?

Car

Baby's Head

Pipe

Puppy Dog